how to...

use the
PSC communication forms
For use with the Professional Services Contract

An NEC document

ɔril 2013

Construction Clients' Board endorsement of NEC3

The Construction Clients' Board recommends that public sector organisations use the NEC3 contracts when procuring construction. Standardising use of this comprehensive suite of contracts should help to deliver efficiencies across the public sector and promote behaviours in line with the principles of *Achieving Excellence in Construction*.

Cabinet Office UK

---

neccontract.com

NEC is a division of Thomas Telford Ltd, which is a wholly owned subsidiary of the Institution of Civil Engineers (ICE), the owner and developer of the NEC.

The NEC is a family of standard contracts, each of which has these characteristics:

- Its use stimulates good management of the relationship between the two parties to the contract and, hence, of the work included in the contract.

- It can be used in a wide variety of commercial situations, for a wide variety of types of work and in any location.

- It is a clear and simple document – using language and a structure which are straightforward and easily understood.

NEC3 how to use the PSC communication forms is one of the NEC family and is consistent with all other NEC3 documents.

ISBN (complete box set) 978 0 7277 5867 5
ISBN (this document) 978 0 7277 5917 7
ISBN (Professional Services Contract) 978 0 7277 5887 3
ISBN (Professional Services Contract Guidance Notes and Flow Charts) 978 0 7277 5913 9
ISBN (how to write the PSC Scope) 978 0 7277 5915 3

British Library Cataloguing in Publication Data for this publication is available from the British Library.

Typeset by Academic + Technical, Bristol

Printed and bound in Great Britain by Bell & Bain Limited, Glasgow, UK

CONTENTS

FOREWORD

I was delighted to be asked to write the Foreword for the NEC3 Contracts.

I have followed the outstanding rise and success of NEC contracts for a number of years now, in particular during my tenure as the 146th President of the Institution of Civil Engineers, 2010/11.

In my position as UK Government's Chief Construction Adviser, I am working with Government and industry to ensure Britain's construction sector is equipped with the knowledge, skills and best practice it needs in its transition to a low carbon economy. I am promoting innovation in the sector, including in particular the use of Building Information Modelling (BIM) in public sector construction procurement; and the synergy and fit with the collaborative nature of NEC contracts is obvious. The Government's construction strategy is a very significant investment and NEC contracts will play an important role in setting high standards of contract preparation, management and the desirable behaviour of our industry.

In the UK, we are faced with having to deliver a 15–20 per cent reduction in the cost to the public sector of construction during the lifetime of this Parliament. Shifting mind-set, attitude and behaviour into best practice NEC processes will go a considerable way to achieving this.

Of course, NEC contracts are used successfully around the world in both public and private sector projects; this trend seems set to continue at an increasing pace. NEC contracts are, according to my good friend and NEC's creator Dr Martin Barnes CBE, about better management of projects. This is quite achievable and I encourage you to understand NEC contracts to the best you can and exploit the potential this offers us all.

Peter Hansford

UK Government's Chief Construction Adviser
Cabinet Office

PREFACE

The NEC contracts are the only suite of standard contracts designed to facilitate and encourage good management of the projects on which they are used. The experience of using NEC contracts around the world is that they really make a difference. Previously, standard contracts were written mainly as legal documents best left in the desk drawer until costly and delaying problems had occurred and there were lengthy arguments about who was to blame.

The language of NEC contracts is clear and simple, and the procedures set out are all designed to stimulate good management. Foresighted collaboration between all the contributors to the project is the aim. The contracts set out how the interfaces between all the organisations involved will be managed – from the client through the designers and main contractors to all the many subcontractors and suppliers.

Versions of the NEC contract are specific to the work of professional service providers such as project managers and designers, to main contractors, to subcontractors and to suppliers. The wide range of situations covered by the contracts means that they do not need to be altered to suit any particular situation.

The NEC contracts are the first to deal specifically and effectively with management of the inevitable risks and uncertainties which are encountered to some extent on all projects. Management of the expected is easy, effective management of the unexpected draws fully on the collaborative approach inherent in the NEC contracts.

Most people working on projects using the NEC contracts for the first time are hugely impressed by the difference between the confrontational characteristics of traditional contracts and the teamwork engendered by the NEC. The NEC does not include specific provisions for dispute avoidance. They are not necessary. Collaborative management itself is designed to avoid disputes and it really works.

It is common for the final account for the work on a project to be settled at the time when the work is finished. The traditional long period of expensive professional work after completion to settle final payments just is not needed.

The NEC contracts are truly a massive change for the better for the industries in which they are used.

Dr Martin Barnes CBE

Originator of the NEC contracts

ACKNOWLEDGEMENTS

The original NEC was designed and drafted by Dr Martin Barnes then of Coopers and Lybrand with the assistance of Professor J. G. Perry then of the University of Birmingham, T.W. Weddell then of Travers Morgan Management, T.H. Nicholson, Consultant to the Institution of Civil Engineers, A Norman then of the University of Manchester Institute of Science and Technology and P.A. Baird then Corporate Contracts Consultant, Eskom, South Africa.

NEC wishes to acknowledge and thank the *how to use the PSC communication forms* project team for their input to this guidance.

The members of the Project team include:

R. A. Gerrard, BSc(Hons), MRICS, FCIArb, FCInstCES
P. Higgins, BSc, CEng, FICE, FCIArb

Part 1 Introduction

NEC3 Contracts require various communications to be given. These might include an instruction, an acceptance or a notification, to name a few. These communications are threaded into the contract processes alongside the obligations of the various parties. For example, clause 32.2 of the NEC3 Professional Service Contract (PSC) states

> **"The *Consultant* submits a revised programme to the *Employer* for acceptance..."**

This clause, read together with clause 31.1 obliges the *Consultant* at different times in the contract to produce a programme, to revise it and submit it for acceptance. The required communication in this clause takes the form of a submission of the revised programme by the *Consultant* to the *Employer*.

In turn, clause 31.3 states

> **"Within two weeks of the *Consultant* submitting a programme to him for acceptance, the *Employer* either accepts the programme or notifies the *Consultant* of his reasons for not accepting it."**

Here, the *Employer* has a certain time period to either accept the programme or notify his reasons for not accepting the programme. The communications here take the form of the *Employer* either be an accepting (the programme) or notifying (that he does not accept the programme, together with reasons).

PSC clause 13.1 details the communications the contract requires to be given, what form they take and what language writing should be in.

> **"Each instruction, certificate, submission, proposal, record, acceptance, notification, reply and other communication which this contract requires is communicated in a form which can be read, copied and recorded. Writing is in the *language of this contract*."**

As stated in the PSC Guidance Notes[1], 'in a form that can be read, copied and recorded' includes a letter sent by post, telex, cable, electronic mail, facsimile transmission, and on disc, magnetic tape or similar electronic means.

In contrast, the short contracts such as the NEC3 Professional Services Short Contract (PSSC) requires

> **"Each communication which this contract requires has effect when it is received in writing at the last address notified by the recipient for receiving communications."**

The PSSC requires the correct communication to be given, such as notifications and acceptances, requires them to be in writing and details when these take effect.

On this basis, NEC produced a number of simple, basic forms for users to better manage their NEC3 Contracts. These do not cover all of the various communication forms that might be required, the intention being that forms for the likely frequent communications are provided but not for the infrequent communications. When using the PSC, *Employer*'s instructions to change the Scope will occur more frequently than a *Consultant*'s proposal, for instance. The instruction form is provided, the proposal form is not but users can adapt those forms they have quite readily to other communication forms as and when required.

Forms are produced for most of the NEC3 Contracts, or can easily be adapted from others, except for the NEC3 Framework Contract and the NEC3 Adjudicator's Contract. Users can take the forms and adapt them to suit their projects as they see fit.

---

[1] NEC3 Professional Services Contract Guidance Notes

Forms available for the NEC3 Term Service Contract (PSC) include:

- *Employer*'s instruction (EI)
- *Employer*'s notification (EN)
- *Consultant*'s notification (CN)
- Payment certificate (PC)
- Completion certificate (CC)

These are shown below.

Employer's Instruction

For use with PSC

To: _____   Date: _____

Project Name: _____   Project ID: _____

Instruction No: _____

Under clause _____ I instruct you to:

_____

_____

_____

_____

_____

_____

_____

Copy to: _____

Signed: _____

For: _____   Date: _____

Employer's **Notification**

For use with PSC

To: _____   Date: _____

Project Name: _____   Project ID: _____

Notification No: _____

Under clause _____ I notify you:

_____

_____

_____

_____

_____

_____

_____

_____

Copy to: _____

Signed: _____

For: _____   Date: _____

Consultant's Notification

For use with PSC

To: Date:

Project Name: Project ID:

Notification No:

Under clause _____ I notify you:

Copy to:

Signed:

For: Date:

how to use the PSC communication forms

Payment Certificate

For use with PSC

To: _____   Date: _____

Project Name: _____   Project ID: _____

Certificate No: _____

Under clause 51.1:

Prices for Services Provided to Date	£ _____
The amount of the *expenses* properly spent by the *Consultant* in Providing the Services	£ _____
Other amounts to be paid to the *Consultant*	£ _____
Sub-total	£ _____
Less amounts to be paid by or retained from the *Consultant*	£ _____
Amount due	£ _____
Less amount due in the last payment certificate	£ _____
Sub-total	£ _____
Tax which the law requires the *Employer* to pay to the *Consultant*	£ _____
Change in the amount due since the last payment certificate which is certified for payment	£ _____

Copy to: _____

Signed: _____

For: _____   Date: _____

Completion Certificate

For use with PSC

To: _____   Date: _____

Project Name: _____   Project ID: _____

Certificate No: _____

Under clause 30.2:

the date of Completion of .... [insert either any *section* of the *services* or the

whole of the *services*] is .... [insert date]

_____

_____

_____

_____

_____

Copy to: _____

Signed: _____

For: _____   Date: _____

These simple NEC communication forms, together with Contract Datas for the NEC3 Contracts, are available as part of the membership of the NEC Users' Group (see www.neccontract.com). Alternatively, these are provided to purchasers of digital NEC3 Contracts.

Users should note that some forms have multiple uses. For example, the *Consultant*'s Notification form can be used to notify matters such as:

- a change of address for receiving communications (clause 13.2),
- early warnings (clause 15.1),
- compensation events (clause 61.3),
- failure of *Employer* in respect of compensation events (clause 61.4, 62.6, 64.4) and
- a dispute (clause W1.3(2)) or intention to refer to *tribunal* (clause W1.4(2) & (3)), (clause W2.4(2)).

Clause 13.7 states

> **"A notification which this contract requires is communicated separately from other communications."**

With the exception of notifications therefore, other communications could be communicated together.

The following parts of this guidance illustrate some completed forms applied to a fictitious project. This is a project management commission and uses the worked example of the PSC Contract Data from the PSC Guidance Notes. This is shown in Appendix 1. The associated example Activity Schedule is shown in Appendix 2.

It is usual to have a start-up meeting where matters such as communications protocol would likely feature. Who is going to act on behalf of the *Consultant* and to whom should communications be sent to? Is the address in Contract Data part two the one to be used for communications? Is there a replacement *Employer's Agent* on this project?

On our project, the *Employer* advised the *Consultant* that a replacement *Employer's Agent* was going to be notified to the *Consultant*, immediately following the start-up meeting. This was due to a long term illness and was notified on EN1.

Employer's **Notification**

To: **Mr M Jones, PM Services Ltd**   Date: **5th July 2013**

Project Name: **Long Acre Works – PM Services**   Project ID: **1234**

Notification No: **1**

Under clause X10.2 I notify you:

that the *Employer's Agent* Mr T. Chimes will be replaced by Mr J. Strummer with

immediate effect. His contact details are ....

Copy to: **Head Office**

Signed:

For: **European Grain plc**   Date: **5th July 2013**

Part 2 Early warnings

Clause 15 deals with early warnings and is designed to be a reciprocal but simple risk management tool. If the *Consultant* or the *Employer* becomes aware of any of the matters stated in clause 15.1 they are obligated to notify an early warning.

> **"The *Employer* and the *Consultant* give an early warning by notifying the other as soon as either becomes aware of any matter which could..."**

The early warning process is entirely separate from the compensation event process. Sometimes matters start out as early warnings and may indeed become compensation events, but often not. When a compensation event arises, the *Employer* and *Consultant* are left only to deal with cost matters arising due to the event. When an early warning matter arises, the *Employer* and *Consultant* set about making and considering proposals for how the effect of the registered risks can be avoided and reduced, amongst other obligations, at risk reduction meetings.

There is little point and no obligation to notify an early warning of a matter which has happened and has no future consequence. The process is about seeking solutions to problems which is therefore to do with the future, not the past. If an event has happened it may well be a compensation event or perhaps a Defect, not something that requires an early warning to be notified.

In our project, the *Consultant* had been advised by the construction contractor that one of the suppliers on the project had gone into administration. The *Consultant* considered this was a matter he was obliged to notify an early warning to the *Employer*. The communication is a notification and comes from the *Consultant* so the *Consultant*'s Notification form is used, as shown below.

Consultant's Notification

To: **Mr J Strummer, European Grain plc**   Date: **8th July 2013**

Project Name: **Long Acre Works – PM Services**   Project ID: **1234**

Notification No: **1**

Under clause 16.1 I notify you:

that XYZ Supplies Ltd you have procured have today gone into administration.

They were providing the free issue signs for the extension works. We were

co-ordinating their supply dates with the works contractor.

Copy to: **Head Office**

Signed:

For: **PM Services Ltd**   Date: **8th July 2013**

On receipt of this notified early warning, the *Employer* realised that he had not put together the first Risk Register and decided to compile this straight away, following the *Consultant's* notified early warning.

The first Risk Register contains all of the matters listed in Contract Data part one and two (shown in Appendix 1), together with the early warning notified by the *Consultant* earlier. The Risk Register is not a contract document, is not in place until after the contract is awarded and is a register that helps promote better management of risks which have not yet been avoided or reduced.

The Risk Register is defined in clause 11.2(10), the first part of the clause states where the risks come from:

> **"The Risk Register is a register of the risks which are listed in the Contract Data and the risks which the *Employer* or the *Consultant* has notified as an early warning matter."**

The second part of the clause states what must be shown on the register:

"It includes a description of the risk and a description of the actions which are to be taken to avoid or reduce the risk."

There is no Risk Register form produced by NEC, many organisations have their own procedures in place for such. This is fine but the parties need to ensure that the requirements of the contract are followed. The *Employer* included the two things stated above that the contract demands, but also added some additional column to suit the project. This is good management – regard the contract as a set of minimum obligations, there is nothing stopping the parties doing more than the minimum required if they feel it is in the interests of the project.

The *Employer* issued the Risk Register to the *Consultant* and instructed the *Consultant* to attend a risk reduction meeting to take place the next day.

Risk Register

To: **Mr M Jones, PM Services Ltd**   Date   **9th July 2013**

Project Name: **Long Acre Works – PM Services**   Project ID: **1234**

Risk Register No: **1**

ID	Source	Description of the risk	Description of the actions to be taken to avoid or reduce the risk	Now been avoided or have passed?
1	CD1	Possible re-configuration of unloading facility		no
2	CD1	Limited car parking availability for *Consultant*'s personnel		no
3	CD1	Possible delays in free-issue permanent facility ABC equipment		no
4	CD2	Onerous take over testing of new facility		no
5	CD2	Concern that construction period of new facility is tight		no

Copy to: **Head Office**

Signed:

For: **European Grain plc**   Date: **9th July 2013**

The *Employer* and the *Consultant* attended the risk reduction meeting. Other people could have attended the meeting if either the *Employer* or *Consultant* considered this would be of benefit. This is detailed in clause 15.2.

At any risk reduction meeting, clause 15.3 requires

> "those who attend co-operate in:
>
> - making and considering proposals for how the effect of the registered risks can be avoided or reduced,
> - seeking solutions that will bring advantage to all those who will be affected,
> - deciding on the actions which will be taken and who, in accordance with this contract, will take them and
> - deciding which risks have now been avoided or have passed and can be removed from the Risk Register."

As shown, there are four basic requirements to work through in any risk reduction meeting. The meeting could last 5 minutes or 5 hours, there could be 2 people or 10, it could be in person, by teleconference or videoconference; the who, how, where, when aspects of the meeting are left to the *Employer* and *Consultant* to apply judgement in deciding what is best in the circumstances.

On our project, the attendees made their decision on CN1. The *Employer* had used a number of sign suppliers in the past and was confident they could procure an alternative supplier very soon. The *Employer* would get his legal advisers to attend to XYZ Supplier Ltd's accounts following the administration.

During the meeting they took the opportunity to address one other matters listed on the Risk Register. These decisions were recorded, the Risk Register was revised and immediately issued to the *Consultant*.

			Risk Register	
To: **Mr M Jones, PM Services Ltd**			Date: **10th July 2013**	
Project Name: **Long Acre Works – PM Services**			Project ID: **1234**	
Risk Register No: **2**				
ID	Source	Description of the risk	Description of the actions to be taken to avoid or reduce the risk	Now been avoided or have passed?
1	CD1	Possible re-configuration of unloading facility		no
2	CD1	Limited car parking availability for *Consultant's* personnel	*Consultant's* personnel will be encouraged to share lifts or get public transport (C)	yes
3	CD1	Possible delays in free-issue permanent facility ABC equipment		no
4	CD2	Onerous take over testing of new facility		no
5	CD2	Concern that construction period of new facility is tight		no
6	CN1	XYZ Supplies in administration	Employer to procure new supplier (E)	no
Copy to: **Head Office**				
Signed:				
For: **European Grain plc**			Date: **10th July 2013**	

This process continues throughout the contract period, early warnings are notified, captured on the Risk Register, risk reduction meetings are held and hopefully most problems are solved bringing advantage to all those who will be affected. The Risk Register is kept up-to-date through the risk reduction meetings and the parties can keep the risks in number ID order, or whether they have been avoided or passed, or by a most sophisticated likelihood/severity method, if they wanted to. There is no prescriptive requirement for such in the PSC, the parties can decide what is best for them.

Part 3 The programme

Clauses 31 and 32 deal with the *Consultant*'s programme. Each programme is submitted to the *Employer* for acceptance, when this happens it becomes the Accepted Programme. Clause 11.2(1) states

> **"The Accepted Programme is the programme identified in the Contract Data or is the latest programme accepted by the *Employer*. The latest programme accepted by the *Employer* supersedes previous Accepted Programmes."**

The programme must show all of the matters stated in clause 31.2 but there is no prescription format the programme itself takes. Quite commonly this might take the form of a Gantt chart with supporting documents, but it could be any number of visual and/or description documentation. The first programme might be identified in the Contract Data, established during the tender period, or if not then is submitted by the *Consultant* within the period stated in the Contract Data.

Within two weeks of the *Consultant* submitting a programme to the *Employer* for acceptance, clause 31.3 states the *Employer* either

> **"accepts the programme or notifies the *Consultant* of his reasons for not accepting it."**

The four stated reasons for the *Employer* to not accept the programme are stated in clause 31.3. When revised programmes are submitted to the *Employer* for acceptance they should show all of the four bulleted requirements stated in clause 32.1 including things such as actual progress achieved, the effects of implemented compensation events and other changes which the *Consultant* proposes to make to the Accepted Programme. The *Employer* again has to then accept or not accept in accordance with clause 31.3. Revised programmes are submitted within the *period for reply* after the *Employer* has instructed the *Consultant* to, when the *Consultant* chooses to and, in any case, at no longer interval stated in the Contract Data from the *starting date* until Completion of the whole of the *services* (clause 32.2). The parties can react to the need to update the programme as they see fit for their project.

In addition to the clause 31/32 provisions for the programme itself, the programme features in a number of PSC processes:

- "The *Employer* and the *Consultant* give an early warning . . . of a matter which could . . . change the **Accepted Programme** . . ." (clause 15.1).
- "If an event occurs which . . . stops the *Consultant* Providing the Service by the date shown on the **Accepted Programme** . . . the *Employer* gives an instruction . . . " (clause 18.1).
- The *Employer* provides information and other things which this contract requires him to provide in accordance with the **Accepted Programme** (clause 20.1).
- The *Employer* provides access to a person, place or thing to the *Consultant* as stated in the Contract Data on or before the later of its *access date* and the access date for it shown on the **Accepted Programme** (clause 25.2).
- "A quotation for an acceleration comprises . . . a revised **programme** . . ." (clause 34.1).
- A compensation event is where "The *Employer* does not provide something which he is to provide by the date for providing it shown on the Accepted Programme" (clause 60.1(3)).
- Further compensation events are where:
  - The *Employer* or Others do not work in accordance with the times shown on the **Accepted Programme** or within the conditions stated in the Scope (clause 60.1(5)).
  - "An event which . . . stops the *Consultant* completing the *services* by the date shown on the **Accepted Programme** . . ." (clause 60.1(11)).

- In any quotation for a compensation event, if "the **programme** for remaining work is altered by the compensation event, the *Consultant* includes the alterations to the **Accepted Programme** in his quotation" (clause 62.2).
- A delay to the Completion Date is assessed as the length of time that, due to the compensation event, planned Completion is later than planned Completion as shown on the **Accepted Programme** (clause 63.3).
- A delay to a Key Date is assessed as the length of time that, due to the compensation event, the planned date when the Condition stated for a Key Date will be met is later than the date shown on the **Accepted Programme** (clause 63.3).
- Assessments (of compensation events) are based upon the assumptions that the *Consultant* will react competently and promptly to the compensation event and that the **Accepted Programme** can be changed (clause 63.7).
- The third of four instances the *Employer* assesses a compensation event is if "...when the *Consultant* submits quotations for a compensation event, he has not submitted a **programme** or alterations to a **programme** which this contract requires him to submit." (clause 64.1).
- The fourth instance is if "...when the *Consultant* submits quotations for a compensation event, the *Employer* has not accepted the *Consultant*'s latest **programme** for one of the reasons stated in this contract" (clause 64.1).
- The *Employer* assesses a compensation event using his own assessment of the programme for the remaining work if there is no **Accepted Programme** or the *Consultant* has not submitted a **programme** or alterations to a **programme** for acceptance as required by this contract (clause 64.2).
- "The *Employer* may terminate the *Consultant*'s obligation to Provide the Services by notifying the *Consultant* if an event occurs which...stops the *Consultant* completing the *services* by the date shown on the **Accepted Programme**..." (clause 90.4).
- The *Consultant* provides information which shows how each activity on the Activity Schedule relates to the operations on each **programme** which he submits for acceptance" (clause 31.4, Option A & C).
- The *Consultant* provides information which shows how each item included in a Task relates to the operations on each **programme** which he submits for acceptance" (clause 31.5, Option G).
- When the *Employer* accepts a quotation for an acceleration, he changes the Prices, the Completion Date and the Key Dates accordingly and accepts the revised **programme** (clause 34.3, Option A & C).
- When the *Employer* accepts a quotation for an acceleration, he changes the Prices, the Completion Date, the Key Dates and the forecast of the total Time Charge for the whole of the *services* accordingly and accepts the revised **programme** (clause 34.3, Option E).
- If the *Consultant* changes a planned method of completing the *services* at his discretion so that the Activity Schedule does not comply with the **Accepted Programme**, he submits a revision of the Activity Schedule to the *Employer* for acceptance (clause 53.2, Option A & C). A reason for not accepting a revision of the Activity Schedule is that "...it does not comply with the **Accepted Programme**..." (clause 53.3, Option A & C).
- "The *Employer* includes the changes to the... **programme** for the Task..." (clause 65.5, Option F).
- The *Consultant* changes his **programme** if it is necessary to do so in order to comply with the revised timetable (clause X12.3(7)).
- "The *Consultant* submits revised **programmes** at intervals no longer than... weeks" (Contract Data part one).
- "The *Consultant* is to submit a first **programme** for acceptance within... weeks of the Contract Date" (Contract Data part one).
- "The **programme** identified in the Contract Data is..." (Contract Data part two).

There is no standard NEC form for a *Consultant*'s submission; this one is created using a template from one of the other forms.

Consultant's Submission

To: **Mr J Strummer, European Grain plc**   Date: **12th July 2013**

Project Name: **Long Acre Works – PM Services**   Project ID: **1234**

Submission No: **1**

I submit the following under clause 31.1:

our first programme for acceptance (ref programme/1), as attached.

Copy to: **Head Office**

Signed:

For: **PM Services Ltd**   Date: **12th July 2013**

Clause 31.3 states

> **"Within two weeks of the *Consultant* submitting a programme to him for acceptance, the *Employer* either accepts the programme or notifies the *Consultant* of his reasons for not accepting it."**

On our project, the *Employer* was satisfied that all of the clause 31.2 requirements had been properly included in the programme, and then issued the following notification. If the *Employer* did not accept the programme, then he would notify the reason for not accepting – four reasons are given to the *Employer* in clause 31.3 for this.

There is no standard NEC form for an *Employer*'s acceptance; this one is created using a template from one of the other forms.

Employer's Acceptance

To: **Mr M Jones, PM Services Ltd**   Date: **15th July 2013**

Project Name: **Long Acre Works – PM Services**   Project ID: **1234**

Acceptance No: **1**

Under clause 31.3 I accept:

your programme ref programme/1 dated 12th July 2013.

Copy to: **Head Office**

Signed:

For: **European Grain plc**   Date: **15th July 2013**

Part 4 Compensation events

Compensation events are events which, if they occur and do not arise from the *Consultant*'s fault, entitle the *Consultant* to be compensated for any effect the event may have on the Prices, the Completion Date and any Key Dates; also to the Task Completion Date ordered under a Task Order if Option G is used. A compensation event will often result in additional payment to the *Consultant* but may result in reduced payment.

Compensation events are listed in the core clauses. Further compensation events are stated in Option G (listing a further three compensation events), Options X2 and X12. The main list is in clause 60.1; this includes events (1) to (12).

There are four parts to the compensation event process within the PSC. These are notification, quotation, assessment and then implementation.

Most compensation events on most contracts will probably arise due to the *Employer* instructing a change to the Scope. On our project, the *Employer* attended a Board meeting where he had been asked to submit a monthly progress report on the extension works. In turn, the *Employer* decided that he should ask the *Consultant* to provide part of this, dealing with construction progress matters. The *Employer* immediately wrote the following instruction:

Employer's **Instruction**

To: **Mr M Jones, PM Services Ltd**　　　Date: **15th July 2013**

Project Name:　**Long Acre Works – PM Services**　　Project ID: **1234**

Instruction No:　**1**

Under clause　20.2　I instruct you to:

produce an electronic monthly progress report in the attached format on the

1st of each month.

Copy to:　**Head Office**

Signed:

For:　　　**European Grain plc**　　　　　Date: **15th July 2013**

Clause 61.1 requires the *Employer* to notify the *Consultant* of a compensation event at the time of giving the instruction. This is quite a novel requirement in standard forms of contract, most expect the *Consultant* to identify change; this reflects the good management required in the PSC.

The notification stage on our project occurs when, at the same time of issuing EI1, the *Employer* notified this as a compensation event. Clause 13.7 requires that a notification which the contract requires is communicated separately from other communications:

Employer's Notification

To: **Mr M Jones, PM Services Ltd**   Date: **15th July 2013**

Project Name: **Long Acre Works – PM Services**   Project ID: **1**

Notification No: **2**

Under clause 61.1 I notify you:

that my instruction EI 1 is a compensation event under clause 60.1(1).

Copy to: **Head Office**

Signed:

For: **European Grain plc**   Date: **15th July 2013**

After giving the instruction and notifying the compensation event, the *Employer* is required to instruct the *Consultant* to submit quotations, unless the event arises from a fault of the *Consultant* or quotations have already been submitted. This is stated in clause 61.1.

Employer's Instruction

To: **Mr M Jones, PM Services Ltd**   Date: **15th July 2013**

Project Name: **Long Acre Works – PM Services**   Project ID: **1234**

Instruction No: **2**

Under clause 61.1 I instruct you to:

submit a quotation for the compensation event that arises from EI1.

Copy to: **Head Office**

Signed:

For: **European Grain plc**   Date: **15th July 2013**

The next stage of the compensation event process is the quotation; this is something for the *Consultant* to prepare and this comprises proposed changes to the Prices, the Completion Date and any Key Dates.

There are a number of provisions within the PSC that the *Consultant* and *Employer* need to be aware of during the preparation of the quotation. These include:

- Alternative quotations may be beneficial (see clause 62.1).
- The *Consultant* should submit details of his assessment with each quotation (see clause 62.2).
- If the programme for remaining work is altered by the compensation event, the *Consultant* includes the alterations to the Accepted Programme in his quotation (see clause 62.2).
- The compensation event should be assessed in accordance with clause 63.1.
- Whether the *Employer* has notified the *Consultant* of his decision that the *Consultant* did not give an early warning of a compensation event which an experienced consultant could have given (see clause 63.5).

- Whether the quotation should make due allowance for any *Consultant*'s risk (see clause 63.6).
- If the compensation event is as a result of an instruction to change the Scope in order to resolve an ambiguity or inconsistency (see clause 63.8).

Once these provisions are considered, the *Consultant* submits the quotation. Clause 62.3 states

> **"The *Consultant* submits quotations within two weeks of being instructed to do so by the *Employer*."**

Consultant's Submission

To: **Mr J Strummer, European Grain plc**   Date: **22nd July 2013**

Project Name: **Long Acre Works – PM Services**   Project ID: **1234**

Submission No: **2**

I submit the following under clause 62.3:

our quotation for EI1 comprises the proposed change to the Prices of £1,800.00,

the details of our assessment is attached. Our programme for the remaining work

is not altered by this compensation event.

Copy to: **Head Office**

Signed:

For: **PM Services Ltd**   Date: **22nd July 2013**

Clause 63.14 states that

> **"Assessments for changed Prices for compensation events are in the form of changes to the Activity Schedule."**

The changes to the Activity Schedule could result in items being modified, added or deleted. This particular compensation event resulted in an item being added to it. The *Consultant* can append the proposed changes to the quotation submission along with details of his assessment and any alterations to the Accepted Programme. As the Activity Schedule is quite small on this project, it is sensible to submit it as a whole, showing the changes. If it were multiple pages, then just stating or showing the proposed changes would be more appropriate. The same consideration is given to the Accepted Programme, where the contract only requires the alterations to be shown.

Activity Schedule

Activity number	Description	Unit	Price (£)
	Provide PM services as stated in Scope part 4		
1	Month 1	sum	7,000
2	Month 2	sum	7,000
3	Month 3	sum	7,000
4	Month 4	sum	7,000
5	Month 5	sum	7,000
6	Month 6	sum	7,000
7	Month 7	sum	7,000
8	Month 8	sum	7,000
8	Month 9	sum	7,000
10	Month 10	sum	7,000
11	Month 11	sum	7,000
12	Month 12	sum	7,000
13	Provide deliverable as Scope part 5.1	sum	6,000
14	Provide deliverable as Scope part 5.2	sum	3,400
	Compensation events		
15	Additional reporting as EI1	sum	1,800
	Total of the Prices		95,200

Upon receipt of the quotation the *Employer*, in accordance with clause 62.3, can instruct the *Consultant* to submit a revised quotation (only after explaining his reasons for doing so), accept this or notify that he will be making his own assessment (which may happen in certain circumstances such as the *Consultant* not submitting a quotation and details of his assessment within the time allowed).

On our project, the *Employer* was happy with how the *Consultant* had assessed the quotation and accepted this (the details were not included here but assume they were assessed by the *Employer*). The way that this particular compensation event is added to the Activity Schedule means that the whole activity must be completed before it is paid for. This could have been a series of activities leading to a series of payments, rather than just the one.

Employer's Notification

To: **Mr M Jones, PM Services Ltd**   Date: **24th July 2013**

Project Name: **Long Acre Works – PM Services**   Project ID: **1234**

Notification No: **3**

Under clause 62.3 I notify you:

that I accept your quotation of £1,800.00 for the EI1 compensation event.

Copy to: **Head Office**

Signed: _____

For: **European Grain plc**   Date: **24th July 2013**

Clause 65.3 states

> **"The changes to the Prices, the Completion Date and the Key Dates are included in the notification implementing a compensation event."**

The *Employer* could append the changed Activity Schedule to the notification implementing a compensation event.

Activity Schedule

Activity number	Description	Unit	Price (£)
	Provide PM services as stated in Scope part 4		
1	Month 1	sum	7,000
2	Month 2	sum	7,000
3	Month 3	sum	7,000
4	Month 4	sum	7,000
5	Month 5	sum	7,000
6	Month 6	sum	7,000
7	Month 7	sum	7,000
8	Month 8	sum	7,000
9	Month 9	sum	7,000
10	Month 10	sum	7,000
11	Month 11	sum	7,000
12	Month 12	sum	7,000
13	Provide deliverable as Scope part 5.1	sum	6,000
14	Provide deliverable as Scope part 5.2	sum	3,400
	Compensation events		
15	Additional reporting as EI1	sum	1,800
	Total of the Prices		95,200

The final stage in the process is the implementation of the compensation event. This is not about implementing perhaps some additional *services* instructed, it is instead concerned with the closure of the compensation event itself and how this changes the Activity Schedule.

Clause 65.1 deals provides three instances when implementation takes place, in this part of our project it is the notification of the acceptance by the *Employer* of the *Consultant*'s quotation (first bullet). Clause 65.2 confirms the finality of the compensation event assessment, it is not to be revised if a forecast upon which it is based is shown by later recorded information to have been wrong.

The PSC comprises a series of selected clauses that need to be read together to make the whole. This can be demonstrated through the following sequence of clauses which get from the initial need to change the Scope, to the payment for such:

- The *Consultant* Provides the Services in accordance with the Scope (clause 21.1).
- The *Employer* may give an instruction to the *Consultant* which changes the Scope (clause 20.2).
- The *Consultant* obeys and instruction which is in accordance with this contract and is given to him by the *Employer* (clause 25.3).
- The *Employer* giving an instruction changing the Scope is a compensation event (clause 60.1(1)).
- The compensation event is implemented when one of three instances occur (clause 65.1).

- Assessments for changed Prices for compensation events are in the form of changes to the Activity Schedule (Option A, clause 63.14).
- The changes to the Prices, the Completion Date and the Key Dates are included in the notification implementing a compensation event (Option A, clause 65.3).
- Information in the Activity Schedule is not Scope (Option A, clause 53.1).
- The amount due includes the Price for Services Provided to Date (clause 50.3) which in turn is defined in Option A11.2(15) as being the total of the Prices for the activities which have been completed. A completed activity is one which is without Defects which would delay immediately following work.

For payment purposes on a PSC Option A contract in particular, it is preferable to reach agreement with compensation event assessments as quickly as the parties can as such events only fall for payment when they are both on the Activity Schedule and completed. This is different to the basis of payment for Options C and E.

Part 5 Payment

The *Employer* is obliged to assess the amount due at each assessment date, as stated in clause 50.1. How the amount due is calculated is stated in clause 50.3. The *Employer* makes the payment within three weeks of receiving the *Consultant*'s invoice, unless there is a different payment stated in the Contract Data.

There is nothing to stop the *Employer* and *Consultant* working together to jointly agree the amount due in accordance with the contract. On our project the parties did just that and the *Employer* issued the following payment certificate, with the *Employer* paying it by the latest date the contract stipulates. The *Consultant* confirmed to the *Employer* that the payment for all services carried out to date was subject to VAT at 20%. In accordance with 50.3, therefore, the *Employer* added 20% to the amount the *Employer* was required to pay.

Payment Certificate

| To: | **Mr M Jones, PM Services Ltd** | Date: | **1st August 2013** |

Project Name: **Long Acre Works – PM Services**   Project ID: **1**

Certificate No: **1**

Under clause 51.1:

Prices for Services Provided to Date	£	**7,000**
Plus other amounts to be paid to the *Consultant*	£	**0**
Sub-total	£	**7,000**
Less amounts to be paid by or retained from the *Consultant*	£	**0**
Amount due	£	**7,000**
Less amount due in the last payment certificate	£	**0**
Sub-total	£	**7,000**
Tax which the law requires the *Employer* to pay to the *Consultant*	£	**1,400**
Change in the amount due since the last payment certificate which is certified for payment	£	**8,400**

Copy to:

Signed:

For: **European Grain plc**   Date: **1st August 2013**

Clause 50.3 states that

"**The amount due is**

- **the Price for Services Provided to Date,**
- **the amount of *expenses* properly spent by the *Consultant* in Providing the Services and**
- **other amounts to be paid to the *Consultant* less amounts to be paid by or retained from the *Consultant*.**"

In turn, the Price for Services Provided to Date in clause 11.2(15) for Option A states that it is

"...the total of the Prices for the activities which have been completed. A completed activity is one which is without Defects which would delay immediately following work."

On our project, there were no other amounts to be paid to the *Consultant*, such as X20 Key Performance Indicators for example. There were also no amounts to be paid by or retained from the *Consultant*, for example uncorrected Defects. At the first assessment date, it is just about which activities on the Activity Schedule have been completed. These were as follows:

Activity Schedule

Activity number	Description	Unit	Price (£)
	Provide PM services as stated in Scope part 4		
1	Month 1	sum	7,000
	Total of the Prices		7,000

Part 6 Task Orders

Task Orders are used to call off work under the PSC when main Option G term contract is chosen. A Task Order is defined in Clause 11.2(24) as

> "...the *Employer*'s instruction to carry out a Task"

and a Task is defined in clause 11.2(21) as

> "...work within the *services* which the *Employer* may instruct the *Consultant* to carry out within a stated period of time".

Clause 55.1 requires the *Employer* to consult with the *Consultant* about the contents of a Task Order before he issues it.

If we assume Option G was used on our project, instead of Option A, and that the *Employer* wanted to instruct some additional *services* that the *Consultant* provides. These *services* were to be started and finished within a quite short space of time and get this done over a weekend which is something not provided for in the Scope. Clause 55.2 provides that the Prices for items in the Task price list which are not taken from the Task Schedule are assessed in the same way as compensation events. The additional weekend work costs the *Consultant* would incur would therefore be dealt with as a compensation event. The *Employer* consulted with the *Consultant* straight away and the following was agreed.

There is no standard NEC form for an *Employer*'s Task Order; this one is created using a template from one of the other forms.

Task Order

To: **Mr M Jones, PM Services Ltd**   Date: **5th November 2013**

Project Name: **Long Acre Works – PM Services**   Project ID: **1234**

Task Order No: **3**

Further to our consultation, under Option G you are instructed to carry out the following Task:

Provide a condition survey:

Type 2 as stated in Scope 1.1 for the following asset …...

Type 3 as stated in Scope 1.2 for the following asset …...

Both to take place 23/24 November 2013.

Priced list of items of work in the Task:
The following items are taken from the Task Schedule

Type 2 condition survey, 1 nr @ £1,000.00	£ **1,000.00**
Type 2 condition survey, 1 nr @ £1,500.00	£ **1,500.00**

The following items have been assessed in the same way as a compensation event

Weekend work costs (details attached)	£ **320.00**
Total of the Prices for the Task	£ **2,820.00**

Task starting date: **23rd November 2013**   Task completion date: **24th November 2013**

Amount of delay damages for the late completion of the Task: £ **Nil** per day

Copy to: **Head Office**

Signed:

For: **European Grain plc**   Date: **5th November 2013**

The assumed Task Schedule on our project could look something like that below; the four activities at the top being the list of *services* the *Employer* expected to need and would ask the *Consultant* to provide. There could then be shown a list of instructed Task Orders – Task Order nr 1 and 2 are shown here. There could then be listed a series of compensation events that occurs to the Tasks. At this stage there is only one compensation event, in this case arising due to *Employer*'s Instruction nr 1 in relation to Task Order nr 1.

Task Schedule

Item number	Description	Unit	Expected quantity	Rate (£)	Price (£)
1	Provide condition survey type 1 as stated in Scope 1.1	nr	50	500	–
2	Provide condition survey type 2 as stated in Scope 1.2	nr	20	1,000	–
3	Provide condition survey type 3 as stated in Scope 1.2	sum	30	1,500	–
4	Attend monthly meetings as stated in Scope 4.2	nr	12	1,000	–
	Task Orders				
	TO nr 1 – 2 condition surveys instructed	sum			2,820
	TO nr 2 – 12 condition surveys instructed	sum			16,000
	Compensation events				
	TO nr 1 – changes to Task Order due to EI 1	sum		653	653
				The total of the Prices	19,473

This updated Task Schedule allows for the changes to be considered when assessing the amount due at each assessment date. There could be a series of Task Orders issued during the term of the contract. The Task Orders could be broken down into more detail on the Task Schedule to allow for a smoother cash flow, rather than just be paid on the basis of completion of the whole Task at each assessment date.

Part 7 Defects

There is a reciprocal obligation until the *defects date* on both the *Employer* and *Consultant* to notify each other of each Defect 'as soon as' they find one. This is as stated in clause 41.1. The definition of a Defect is stated in clause 11.2(5) which states

> **"A Defect is a part of the *services* which is not in accordance with the Scope or the applicable law."**

Clause 41.2 states

> **"The *Consultant* corrects a Defect whether or not the *Employer* notifies him of it."**

On our project, the *Consultant* notified the *Employer* of the following Defect:

Consultant's **Notification**

To: **Mr J Strummer, European Grain plc**   Date: **25th November 2013**

Project Name: **Long Acre Works – PM Services**   Project ID: **1234**

Notification No: **2**

Under clause **42.1** you are notified:

we have provided the deliverable as Scope part 5 but have since found an error in

our computer model. This is a Defect. We do not expect this to be significant but

we are correcting this fault now and expect to correct the Defect and re-issue the

deliverable in the next few days.

Copy to: **Head Office**

Signed:

For: **PM Services Ltd**   Date: **25th November 2013**

Clause 41.2 states that it is for the *Consultant* to correct a Defect

"...within a time which minimises the adverse effect on the *Employer* or Others."

In the *Consultant's* notification, one imagines that the proposed time to correct the notified Defect was acceptable. If the *Consultant* does not correct a Defect within the time required by the contract then clause 41.2 states it is for the *Employer* to assess

"...the cost to him of having the Defect corrected by other people and the *Consultant* pays this amount."

The Defect process is quite a simple one, it involves notification then the Defect is either corrected or the financial consequence of an uncorrected Defect is dealt with.

Part 8 Managing communications

In the Introduction to this guide it is states 'NEC3 Contracts require various communications to be given'. These can be both various and sometimes quite extensive. Consider a PSC Option A contract with a well written Scope, minimal instructed change to it and minimal problems that arise through the early warning process. In this case, the number of communications might be quite minimal. Contrast this with a PSC Option E with a developing Scope undergoing constantly instructed change, along with considerable problems that arise through the early warning process. Here, the number of communications could be quite extensive.

Users will therefore need to consider a number of factors when deciding the communication system that is appropriate for their needs. On a PSC contract, the following should be considered:

- Which main Option is it and what would be the communication implications of each?
- How clearly defined is the Scope, what degree of change to this is likely?
- Do the *Employer/Consultant* already have appropriate systems in place?
- What is the extent of risks acting on the project?

This consideration will help shape the appropriate communication system for the project, which could range from a manual based system, using the simple NEC3 contract communication forms used in this guide, through to one of a number of technology based process systems available to users. More details on the technology systems can be found on www.neccontract.com. If the manual based system, then consider putting together a schedule to record and reconcile communications. This would ensure the simple consecutive numbering system is correctly maintained as well as link different communications related to the same subject.

To finish, below are a few useful tips for users to help comply with the PSC requirements for communications:

- Follow the processes carefully – use 'notify', 'accept', 'instruct' etc as the particular clause requires.
- Decide if a manual system or technology based system is best for the project.
- If manual system, agree whether the simple NEC communication forms will be used, add to them if needed, create others if needed; fill in the repetitive data; decide on a tracker schedule.
- If technology based system, which one is best for your particular requirements?
- Finally and when completing the communication forms, use the language of the contract, present tense, plain English.

Appendix 1 Contract Data

CONTRACT DATA
Part one – Data provided by the *Employer*

1 GENERAL

- The *conditions of contract* are the core clauses and the clauses for main Option **A**, dispute resolution Option **W2** and secondary Options **X3, X4, X8, X9, X10, X11, X20, Y(UK)2 and Z** of the NEC3 Professional Services Contract (April 2013).

- The *Employer* is

  Name   **European Grain plc**

- Address   **Long Acre Industrial Estate, Spearshead, Bristol BS8 2LR**
             Tel 01234 567890

- The *Adjudicator* is

  Name   **Mr I Judge**

  Address   **Test House, Micklemersh, Hampshire**

- The *services* are

  Project management of extensions to unloading and distribution facilities at Long Acre Works

- The Scope is in **document ref XX90**.

- The *language of this contract* is **English**.

- The *law of the contract* is the law of **England and Wales**.

- The *period for reply* is **2** weeks.

- The *period for retention* is **2** years following Completion or earlier termination.

- The *Adjudicator nominating body* is **Institution of Civil Engineers**.

- The *tribunal* is **arbitration**.

- The following matters will be included in the Risk Register

  As shown in Document ref XYZ dated 20 June 2013

2 THE PARTIES' MAIN RESPONSIBILITIES

- The *Employer* provides access to the following persons, places and things

- access to   *access date*

  Long Acre Works and *Employer*'s Agent   5 July 2013

- The *Consultant* prepares forecasts of the total *expenses* at intervals no longer than **12** weeks.

3 TIME

- The *starting date* is **5 July 2013**.
- The *Consultant* submits revised programmes at intervals no longer than **5** weeks.
- The *completion date* for the whole of the *services* is **30 June 2014**.
- The *Consultant* is to submit a first programme for acceptance within **3** weeks of the Contract Date.

4 QUALITY

- The quality policy statement and quality plan are provided within **3** weeks of the Contract Date.
- The *defects date* is **26** weeks after Completion of the whole of the *services*.

5 PAYMENT

- The *assessment interval* is **a calendar month**.
- The *currency of this contract* is **pounds sterling (£)**.
- The *interest rate* is **2** % per annum (not less than 2) above the **base lending** rate of **Lloyds Bank plc**
- The *expenses* stated by the *Employer* are

item	amount
car mileage	**40p per mile**
rail travel	**standard class fare**.

8 INDEMNITY, INSURANCE AND LIABILITY

- The amounts of insurance and the periods for which the *Consultant* maintains insurance are

event	cover	period following Completion of the whole of the *services* or earlier termination
failure of the *Consultant* to use the skill and care normally used by professionals providing services similar to the *services*	**£1m** in respect of each claim, without limit to the number of claims	**6 years**
death of or bodily injury to a person (not an employee of the *Consultant*) or loss of or damage to property resulting from an action or failure to take action by the *Consultant*	**£5m** in respect of each claim, without limit to the number of claims	**12 months**
death of or bodily injury to employees of the *Consultant* arising out of and in the course of their employment in connection with this contract	**£2m** in respect of each claim, without limit to the number of claims	**12 months**

- The *Employer* provides the following insurances.

  Liability for loss of or damage to property (except survey equipment) provided by the *Employer* for the use of the *Consultant*. Cover to be the replacement cost until the property is returned to the *Employer*.

- The *Consultant* provides these additional insurances.

  1. Insurance against **liability for loss of or damage to survey equipment provided by the *Employer*.**

- Cover is **replacement cost**.

- Period of cover **until all the equipment is returned to the *Employer*.**

- Deductibles are **nil**.

- The *Consultant*'s total liability to the *Employer* for all matters arising under or in connection with this contract, other than the excluded matters, is limited to **£1,000,000 (one million pounds only)**.

Option W2

- The *arbitration procedure* is

  the latest version of the Institution of Civil Engineers Arbitration Procedure or any amendment or modification in force when the arbitrator is appointed.

- The place where arbitration is to be held is **London**.

- The person or organisation who will choose an arbitrator

  - if the Parties cannot agree a choice or

  - if the *arbitration procedure* does not state who selects an arbitrator is **The Institution of Civil Engineers.**

Option X3

- The *Employer* will pay for the items or activities listed below in the currencies stated

items and activities	other currency	total maximum payment in the currency
1 **Consultancy on design of loading equipment**	**Euros**	**Euros 30,000**
2 _____	_____	_____
3 _____	_____	_____

- The *exchange rates* are those published in **Financial Times** on **1 June 2013**.

Option X8

- The *collateral warranty agreements* are

agreement reference	third party
NXT/Door-1	**Adjacent Properties plc**
_____	_____

Option X10

- The *Employer's Agent* is

  Name   **Mr T. Chimes**

  Address   **Long Acre Industrial Estate, Spearshead, Bristol BS8 2LR**

- The authority of the *Employer's Agent* is **all actions by the *Employer* stated in this contract except clause 51.**

Option X20

- The *incentive schedule* for Key Performance Indicators is in **IS1**.
- A report of performance against each Key Performance Indicator is provided at intervals of **3** months.

Option Z

- The *additional conditions of contract* are **Clauses Z1 to Z6 as in document Grain Additional GA 12 dated 20 June 2013**.

Part two – Data provided by the *Consultant*

- The *Consultant* is

  Name **PM Services Ltd**

  Address **Enterprise Way, Bristol BS90 6PM**

- The *key people* are

  (1) Name **Mr M. Jones**

  Job **Project Manager**

  Responsibilities **In charge of the project**

  Qualifications **MSc, MIMechE**

  Experience **3 years as Project Manager, 4 years as Assistant PM**

  (2) Name **Mr V. Green**

  Job **Chief Designer**

  Responsibilities **Supervising design of plant**

  Qualifications **PhD, FICE**

  Experience **10 years design of process plants**

- The *staff rates* are

name/designation	rate
Mr M. Jones (PM)	**£75 per hour**
Mr T. Headon (Chief Designer)	**£65 per hour**
Ms P. Simonon (Planner)	**£60 per hour**
Assistants	**£35 per hour**

- The following matters will be included in the Risk Register

  As shown in document RR1.

OTHER STATEMENTS

- The *expenses* stated by the *Consultant* are

item	amount
Subsistence (as authorised away from home address)	**£80 per night**
Printing of drawings	**£5.50 per A1 size print**

- The *activity schedule* is **AS/1**.

- The tendered total of the Prices is **£93,400 (ninety three thousand four hundred pounds sterling)**.

Appendix 2 Activity Schedule

The lump sum prices entered for each activity includes for all work and other things necessary to complete the item.

Activity Schedule

Activity number	Description	Unit	Price (£)
	Provide PM services as stated in Scope part 4		
1	Month 1	sum	7,000
2	Month 2	sum	7,000
3	Month 3	sum	7,000
4	Month 4	sum	7,000
5	Month 5	sum	7,000
6	Month 6	sum	7,000
7	Month 7	sum	7,000
8	Month 8	sum	7,000
8	Month 9	sum	7,000
10	Month 10	sum	7,000
11	Month 11	sum	7,000
12	Month 12	sum	7,000
13	Provide deliverable as Scope part 5.1	sum	6,000
14	Provide deliverable as Scope part 5.2	sum	3,400
	Total of the Prices		93,400